**For all portable keyboards by *Kenneth Baker*.**

# THE COMPLETE KEYBOARD PLAYER

## OMNIBUS EDITION

Welcome to the fascinating world of
home music-making.

This course has been written to
help you get the best out of your
electronic keyboard. It will be of great
use to teachers, both private and classroom.

# BOOK 1

By the end of Book 1 you will be:
- Reading music.
- Playing popular melodies in many different styles.
- Adding complete accompaniments, consisting of bass notes, chords and drums, to your songs.
- Creating a wealth of fascinating sounds.

Two helpful features of Book 1 are the peel-off stickers,
which adhere to your keys to remind you of the names of the notes,
and the optional CD or cassette, on which you can hear the author playing all
the songs from the book.

Exclusive Distributors:
**Music Sales Limited**
8/9 Frith Street, London W1V 5TZ, England.
**Music Sales Pty Limited**
120 Rothschild Avenue, Rosebery, NSW 2018, Australia.

This book © Copyright 1994 by
Wise Publications
Order No. AM91807 (Comb-bound edition: AM91774)
ISBN 0-7119-3921-7 (Comb-bound edition: 0-7119-3898-9)

**Your Guarantee of Quality**
As publishers, we strive to produce every book to the
highest commercial standards.
Throughout, the printing and binding have been planned to ensure a sturdy,
attractive publication which should give years of enjoyment.
If your copy fails to meet our high standards, please inform us and
we will gladly replace it.

Music Sales' complete catalogue describes thousands of titles and is
available in full colour sections by subject, direct from Music Sales Limited.
Please state your areas of interest and send a cheque/postal order for £1.50 for postage to:
Music Sales Limited, Newmarket Road, Bury St. Edmunds,
Suffolk IP33 3YB.

Wise Publications
London/New York/Paris/Sydney/Copenhagen/Madrid

# BOOK 1

# BOOK 2

# BOOK 3

# YOUR KEYBOARD

Although the actual layout of modern keyboards varies from model to model, the following features are standard:-

| Power (Mains) | Master Volume | Auto-accompaniment | Voices | Rhythm |
|---|---|---|---|---|
| ■ on / off | max. / min. | ■ normal (off)<br>■ fingered (chords)<br>■ single-finger (chords) | ■ flute<br>■ piano<br>■ violin<br>■ trumpet<br>■ guitar | ■ rock<br>■ swing<br>■ march<br>■ waltz<br>■ bossa nova |

## POWER (MAINS)

Turns the keyboard on or off. Most keyboards can run on batteries or from the mains, using a suitable transformer (see your owner's manual).

## MASTER VOLUME

Controls the overall "loudness" of the instrument.
Usually in the form of a "slider", which can be set anywhere from "minimum" to "maximum".

## AUTO-ACCOMPANIMENT

Adds an accompaniment to your melody – AUTOMATICALLY.

## VOICES (INSTRUMENTS, ORCHESTRA, SOLO)

A selection of sounds and effects to add colour to your melody.

## RHYTHM

Adds drums to your performance.

# SITTING AT YOUR KEYBOARD

Set up your keyboard on its own stand or on a table of medium height. Sit facing the centre of the instrument and adjust your seat so that your arms are level with the keyboard, or sloping down slightly towards it:-

Support your hands from the wrists. Imagine that you are holding a rather fragile ball, and curve your fingers lightly around it:-

With the tips of your fingers cover any five adjacent white notes in each hand:-

This is your normal, most relaxed playing position. After all fingering and hand changes during a piece, you should return to this position.

# FINGER NUMBERS

Your fingers are numbered OUTWARDS from the thumbs, like this:-

L.H. (Left Hand)

R.H. (Right Hand)

# WARM UP

Switch on your keyboard now and turn up the Master Volume control to about halfway. Locate your AUTO section (could be called "Auto Bass Chord", or "Auto-accompaniment") and switch it to NORMAL or OFF:-

Check that you have a sound on your keyboard (any sound will do ). If there is no sound, check that all subsidiary volume controls are up. Run the back of your right hand along the keys from left to right, and note the sounds progressing from LOW to HIGH.
Now run your right hand thumb nail along the keys in the opposite direction (from right to left), and note the sounds progressing from HIGH to LOW.
Locate your VOICES (INSTRUMENTS) section, and select "piano":-

Play a few notes at random and listen to the sound of the piano.
Try adding any special "effects" you might have, such as:-

## VIBRATO

An oscillation, or "wobble" of the note(s).

## REVERBERATION (REVERB)

Adds "echo".

## SUSTAIN

Causes the note(s) to ring on.

## STEREO (or STEREO CHORUS)

Transfers the sound rapidly from speaker to speaker.

Experiment with other voices in the same way.

Note that the "violin" sounds best in the upper part of the keyboard, because this is where a real violin would play, whilst the "trombone" – to be realistic – needs to be played in the low to middle register.

# NOW LET'S PLAY RHYTHM

Your keyboard has a built in drummer, and he's raring to go! There are various rhythms available to you, such as ROCK, SWING, BOSSA NOVA, MARCH, POP, WALTZ, etc. These rhythms can run at virtually any speed (tempo), all controlled by you.
In your RHYTHM or STYLE section now, select ROCK, and press the start button:-

Listen to this Rock rhythm for a while, then try speeding it up and slowing it down, using your TEMPO control (sometimes marked simply:  **+**  and  **−** ).

Press another rhythm button now, say SWING, and hear the rhythm pattern change. Speed up and slow down this Swing rhythm ad lib., then stop it, by pressing the START button again.

# SYNCHRO-START*

This is another, very useful method of starting the drums. Locate and press your SYNCHRO-START button now. Nothing will happen at first (though you may see a flashing light, indicating the speed of the rhythm that is to come).

Play any note in the bottom left hand section of your keyboard, and your drummer will start to play. Stop the rhythm by pressing the START button again.

* Not all keyboards have "synchro-start".

# 3

## BLACK AND WHITE NOTES

Your keyboard has a number of black and white keys\*. The black keys are divided into groups of twos and threes, and these same groups repeat all along the keyboard:-

You need these black key groups to locate the white notes.

## YOUR FIRST WHITE NOTE: C

C is a very commonly used white note. The C's lie directly to the left of each of the "two blacks":-

Punch out your C "stickers" now (included with this book), and place one, without sticking it, on each of your C notes.

Check the position of these C's in relation to the groups of two black notes, then remove the stickers and see if you can locate the C's without them.

## THE OTHER WHITE NOTES

The musical alphabet runs from A to G, and then repeats itself over and over again.
So there are **ONLY SEVEN WHITE NOTES TO LEARN**:-

\*The exact number of keys varies from model to model.

# YOUR SECOND WHITE NOTE: G

The G notes lie here, within the "three" black note groups:-

Punch out your G stickers now, and place them (without sticking) on all the G notes. Check out their position, then remove the stickers and locate all the G's without them.

# 4 SPLITTING THE KEYBOARD

Return to your AUTO section again, and switch on "single-finger chords".

Your keyboard is now divided into two distinct sections:-

A **MELODY** section

An **ACCOMPANIMENT** section

# ACCOMPANIMENT SECTION

The Accompaniment Section of your keyboard is situated at the bottom end (left hand side) of your keyboard. It has note names (letters) printed above it, with an arrow, or bracket, to show where the section ends*. Check to see that you have "single-finger chords" selected, then play any note in your accompaniment section, using your left hand (finger 2, say). You are now hearing a CHORD (three notes playing together), plus (probably), a single bass note.

Play a few more single notes at random in your accompaniment section and listen to the sounds of the chords which your keyboard is producing automatically.

(NOTE: You may have to activate your Rhythm Section to make these single-finger chords work. If so, select any rhythm, say "rock", and press START.)

## C AND G CHORDS

Now, in your accompaniment section, let's learn two specific chords. Do you remember how the note "C" looks, in relation to its two adjacent black keys?

Check that you still have "single-finger chords" set on your keyboard, then play the UPPER C, shown above, with your left hand 2nd finger:-

* The extent of the accompaniment section can vary from model to model.

You can check your C with the letters printed on the fascia of the keyboard.

You are now playing a chord of C, which is written in a box, like this:- C

Do you remember how "G" looks, in relation to its three neighbouring black keys?

Play the LOWER G (shown above) with your left hand 5th finger:-

Check your G against the letters on the fascia.

You are now playing a chord of G, written like this:- G

# 5 ADDING RHYTHM TO YOUR CHORDS

In the RHYTHM section of your keyboard, set "Rock" and "Synchro-start".
(Leave single-finger chords set in the AUTO section.) In the Accompaniment Section
of your keyboard, play C with your left hand 2nd finger:-

└── accompaniment section ──┘

**Left Hand**

As soon as you play this C note the Rock
rhythm will start and you will hear a full
acompaniment, consisting of:-

**BASS LINE**

**CHORDS**

**DRUMS**

Now play note G, with your left hand 5th finger:-

└── accompaniment section ──┘

**Left Hand**

The accompaniment pattern will now change to a chord of G . Listen to this new chord
for a while, then change back to C . Feel free to lift your finger once you have played
each chord note. The rhythm will continue indefinitely while you get ready for the next
chord note. Try a new rhythm pattern now, say "Bossa Nova", and alternate between the
two chords, C and G at your leisure.

# 6  BEATS AND BARS

When you were playing there did you feel the natural pulse of the music?
Underlying most popular music there are pulses, or "beats", which have a regularly recurring accent:-

```
beats:-  1   2   3   4   1   2   3   4   1   2   3   4   (etc.)
         >               >               >
```

When writing this down, vertical lines, called "bar lines", are placed in front of each accented beat:-

```
beats:-  |1   2   3   4   |1   2   3   4   |1   2   3   4   |  (etc.)
          >                >                >
          ↑                ↑                ↑                ↑
       bar lines
```

As well as denoting the natural accents of the piece, these bar lines divide the music up into "bars", or "measures":-

```
         bar (measure) 1        bar 2             bar 3
beats:-  |1   2   3   4   |1   2   3   4   |1   2   3   4   |  (etc.)
          >                >                >
```

# SPACEMAN – ACCOMPANIMENT

Here is your first piece:-

## SPACEMAN

**Single-finger chords**: on
**Rhythm**: rock
**Tempo**: medium

```
        C  finger 2    G  finger 5    C              G
beats:  ‖: 1  2  3  4  |1  2  3  4  |1  2  3  4  |1  2  3  4  :‖
                                                              ↑
                                                      REPEAT SIGN
                                              (go back to the opposite
                                               facing sign, and repeat)
```

For the accompaniment to this piece you need two chords: C and G . They are to be played in the ACOMPANIMENT SECTION of your keyboard, with your left hand, finger 2 on C , finger 5 on G . You hold the C chord for one bar (4 beats), then change to a G chord for one bar, then go back to a C chord for one bar, and so on. If you have the audio which accompanies this book, listen to "SPACEMAN – ACCOMPANIMENT" now.

13

# 7 SPLITTING THE KEYBOARD 2 – THE MELODY SECTION

As you learnt earlier, when you select "single-finger chords" in your AUTO section, you split your keyboard into two sections:-

single-finger chords: on

└─ accompaniment section ─┘└─ melody section ─┘

In the MELODY SECTION (which usually begins at G, but can vary from model to model – see your Owner's Manual), you play the MELODY, or TUNE of the piece, with your right hand. The Voices, or Instruments (flute, piano, violin, etc.), apply only to the MELODY SECTION, since, when the keyboard is split, the Accompaniment Section has a fixed sound.

## *SPACEMAN* – MELODY

This first simple melody consists of only two notes: C and G. In your "voices" section select some kind of "spacey" sound, such as COSMIC, or SYNTH.

## SPACEMAN

As you see, the C note is played four times, then the G note is played four times. This is then repeated on the various higher C's and G's, right to the top of the keyboard, then down again. To save complications, use your right hand finger 2 throughout. Start on your most central C (MIDDLE C), and finish on the G immediately to its right:-

Don't forget, you will be adding an accompaniment later, so *PLAY RHYTHMICALLY.*

If you have the audio which accompanies this book, listen to *"SPACEMAN –MELODY"* now.

# SPACEMAN – BOTH HANDS

Now that you can play both the accompaniment and melody of *Spaceman*, try the piece with both hands together.

Here it is written out in simple form:-

## SPACEMAN Kenneth Baker

**Suggested registration (sound setting):** cosmic or synth

**Rhythm:** rock
**Tempo:** medium
**Single-finger chords:** on

If you have the audio which accompanies this book, listen to *"SPACEMAN – BOTH HANDS"* now.

# SPACEMAN – VARIATION

This time, in the melody of *Spaceman*, instead of "jumping" from C to G, then G to C, and so on, you are going to SLIDE:-

## SPACEMAN Kenneth Baker

Play your four C's as before, then turn your right hand 2nd finger over, and slide rapidly up the intervening white notes until you reach G. Play the four G's as written, then slide up again to the next C, and so on. This sliding technique is called a GLISSANDO (Gliss. for short). On the way down the keyboard you will probably have to change your finger angle to do the glissandi, or, if you wish, you can use your right thumb nail instead.

If you have the audio which accompanies this book, listen to *"SPACEMAN – VARIATION"* now.

# *WHITE ROSE OF ATHENS* – ACCOMPANIMENT

The accompaniment to this song uses the same two chords as *Spaceman*: C and G, but each chord lasts longer:-

## WHITE ROSE OF ATHENS

Words by Norman Newell. Music by Manos Hadjidakis. Additional words by Archie Bleyer

**Single-finger chords:** on
**Rhythm:** 8 beat
**Tempo:** fairly fast
**Synchro-start:** on

C finger 2                                   G finger 5

beats:   | 1   2   3   4  | 1   2   3   4  | 1   2   3   4  | 1   2   3   4  |

                                            C

         | 1   2   3   4  | 1   2   3   4  | 1   2   3   4  | 1   2   3   4  |

                                            G

         | 1   2   3   4  | 1   2   3   4  | 1   2   3   4  | 1   2   3   4  |

                                            C

         | 1   2   3   4  | 1   2   3   4  | 1   2   3   4  | 1   2   3   4  ||

Set up your keyboard as shown above (single-finger chords: on, etc.). Play the first chord C in your Accompaniment Section. The rhythm will start automatically, due to the "synchro-start". Count the beats, following the natural pulse of the music. After two bars (8 beats in all), change to a chord of G and allow this chord to continue for a further FOUR bars (16 beats in all). After that change back to C for a further four bars, and so-on, to the end of the song.

If you have the audio which accompanies this book, listen to *"WHITE ROSE OF ATHENS – ACCOMPANIMENT"* now.

# *WHITE ROSE OF ATHENS* – MELODY

To play the melody of *White Rose Of Athens* you need the following five notes:-

MIDDLE
|C |D |E |F |G
———————————— melody section ————————————

Right
Hand

You may place stickers on these five notes if you wish.

Here are those notes written:-

**TREBLE CLEF**
(used for right hand notes)

**STAVE**
(5 horizontal lines)

As you see, the five notes, which are next door on the keyboard, climb up a sort of musical ladder, using various rungs and the spaces in between them. MIDDLE C is a rather low note, and since there are only five rungs available on the stave, MIDDLE C has to stand below the stave on a little rung of its own. These little rungs (drawn above or below the stave as necessary) are called "Ledger Lines".

Here now is a simplified version of *White Rose Of Athens,* written down in musical notation:

# WHITE ROSE OF ATHENS

Words by Norman Newell. Music by Manos Hadjidakis. Additional words by Archie Bleyer

**Suggested registration:** bouzouki (or guitar)

This song starts on MIDDLE C, played with your right thumb (finger 1). The Middle C note plays six times in all, then the melody moves up by step (i.e. line, to space, to line) through "D" and "E", returning then to the D note, which plays eight times. The second half of the song is similar to the first.

Work through the above version of *White Rose Of Athens* in your own time, noticing all the repeated notes, and the various movements up or down "by step", then listen to this song on your audio (if you have one) to compare results.

# 11 LONG AND SHORT NOTES

In *Spaceman*, and the previous "simplified" version of *White Rose Of Athens*, all the melody notes were the same length, and followed the beat exactly. These "beat" notes, called "quarter notes" or "crotchets", are written like this:-

## WHITE ROSE OF ATHENS

However, tunes do not slavishly follow the beat like this as a rule: to make things more interesting they employ a mixture of LONG and SHORT notes:-

### TIME NOTE CHART

| | | |
|---|---|---|
| ♩ or 𝅘𝅥 | quarter note (crotchet) | 1 beat |
| 𝅗𝅥 or 𝆺 | half note (minim) | hold for 2 beats |
| 𝅗𝅥. or 𝆺. | dotted half note (dotted minim) | hold for 3 beats |
| 𝅝 | whole note (semibreve) | hold for 4 beats |

In the final, correct version of *White Rose Of Athens* (page 19), some of the melody notes must be held down LONGER:-

## WHITE ROSE OF ATHENS

In BAR 1, above, the "C" note is played on beat 1, then held down for a further two beats (beats 2 and 3), while in BAR 3, above, the "D" note is played on beat 1, then held down for a further SEVEN beats, making 8 beats in all. This extension of the "D" note is made possible by the use of a "tie" – a curved line joining two (or more) notes of the same pitch (two "D's", two "E's", etc.).

Work through the whole of *White Rose Of Athens*, (on page 19) now, right hand only, counting your beats and striking or holding down your notes as indicated by the music. When you have mastered the right hand, add the left hand chords and listen to your audio (if you have one) to check your results.

# WHITE ROSE OF ATHENS

Words by Norman Newell. Music by Manos Hadjidakis.
Additional words by Archie Bleyer.

**Suggested registration:** bouzouki (or guitar)

**Rhythm:** 8 beat
**Tempo:** fairly fast ( ♩ = 116 ) *
Synchro-start: on

*__METRONOME MARKING.__ A metronome is an instrument which indicates the speed (tempo) of a piece of music. Some modern keyboards have a metronome built in. If yours doesn't, you can buy a metronome, if you wish, from your local music dealer.

# FINGERED CHORDS

Although it is entirely up to you, it would probably be better in the long run to learn to form real chords in your left hand. To do this switch on FINGERED (CHORDS) in your Auto Accompaniment section, and play as follows:-

FINGERED CHORDS: ON

Practise moving from C to G and back, using the correct fingers, as shown. Since the bottom note, G, is common to both chords, it is good practice to hold it down during the changes.

With Rock rhythm selected, press rhythm START and change your chord on each beat 1, like this:-

**Rhythm:** rock
**Tempo:** medium
(♩ = 112)

count:

## NEW CHORD: F

**single-finger method**
SINGLE-FINGER CHORDS: ON

F

**fingered chord method**
FINGERED CHORDS: ON

F

Practise moving from [F] to [C] and back, first without rhythm, then with rhythm:-

**Rhythm:** rock
**Tempo:** medium
( ♩ = 112)

count: ‖: 4/4   [F]  1  2  3  4  | [C]  1  2  3  4  | [F]  1  2  3  4  | [C]  1  2  3  4  :‖

When playing as "fingered" chords, hold down the middle note, C, throughout.

Now practise moving through [F] , [C] , and [G] , like this:-

**Rhythm:** rock
**Tempo:** medium
( ♩ = 112)

count: ‖: 4/4   [F]  1  2  3  4  | [C]  1  2  3  4  | [G]  1  2  3  4  | [C]  1  2  3  4  :‖

The next two songs: *Bye Bye Love*, and *World*, were big hits for the Everly Brothers, and the Bee Gees respectively. Both songs feature the new chord, [F] . Practise left and right hands separately, first without rhythm, then with rhythm. When you are totally proficient, put both hands together.

# MUSICAL TIES

As we saw in *White Rose Of Athens*, page 18 ff., any note(s) in music may be made to last longer by the use of a TIE. You meet ties next in *World*:-

## WORLD (page 23)

Play the C note on beat 1, then hold it down for two whole bars (eight beats in all).

# PLAYING *LEGATO*

LEGATO is an Italian word, meaning "smooth", "joined up". As you play through the melodies of the next two songs, walk very precisely from finger to finger, releasing the old finger EXACTLY as the new finger goes down. There should be no breaks in sound between the notes, nor ugly overlaps either. This joined-up style of playing is called LEGATO. You always play legato, unless the music is marked otherwise.

# BYE BYE LOVE

Words & Music by Felice and Boudleaux Bryant

**Suggested registration:** clarinet

**Rhythm:** swing
**Tempo:** medium ( ♩ = 132)
Synchro-start: on

# WORLD

Words & Music by Barry Gibb, Robin Gibb and Maurice Gibb

**Suggested registration:** horn

**Rhythm:** rock
**Tempo:** medium ( ♩ = 112)
Synchro-start: on

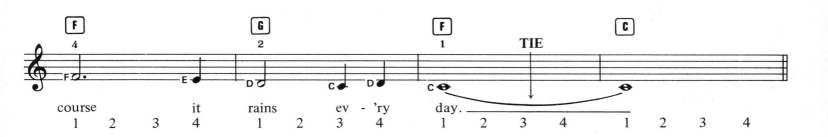

# 13 PICK-UP NOTES

Songs do not always begin on beat 1. In your next song, *One More Night*, by Phil Collins, the melody actually begins on beat 2:-

## ONE MORE NIGHT (page 25)

The three preliminary notes at the beginning of *One More Night* are called PICK-UP NOTES. Beats missing from the pick-up bar appear (usually) in the last bar of the song:-

## ONE MORE NIGHT (end)

This means that you can go around the song again if you wish, keeping the beats intact.

**NOTE:** It is usual to play "no chord" (written N.C.) during pick-up notes.

# ONE MORE NIGHT

Words & Music by Phil Collins

**Suggested registration:** *guitar*

**Rhythm:** rock
**Tempo:** quite slow (♩ = 92)
**Synchro-start:** on

# THREE NEW NOTES: A, B, C, FOR RIGHT HAND

## FINGERING THE NEW NOTES

Now that you are moving beyond the original playing range of your five fingers, new fingering techniques will have to be adopted if the music is to remain LEGATO.

## BLOWIN' IN THE WIND (page 29, last two bars)

Don't jump here; STRETCH OUT for the high C.

## OH, LONESOME ME (page 30, bars 9, 10 and 11)

After playing the last "G" in bar 9, squeeze your hand together in order to get your thumb onto the next note, E. Now STRETCH OUT to encompass the next two notes (G and C).

As soon as you have completed any stretching movements in a song, let your hand return to its normal, relaxed five finger playing position (see picture on page 5).

# RESTS

Silences are often called for in music. In order to indicate these, symbols called "rests" are used. Each of the Time Notes has its own rest:-

| TIME NOTE | | REST (SILENCE) | LASTING |
|---|---|---|---|
| ♩ | quarter note (crotchet) | 𝄽 | 1 beat |
| ♩ | half note (minim) | ▬ | 2 beats |
| ♩. | dotted half note (dotted minim) | ▬• | 3 beats |
| 𝅝 | whole note (semibreve) | ▬ | 4 beats, or one whole bar, regardless of time signature. |

Rests are used mainly for musical or dramatic reasons. However, they are also useful for moving your hand from one part of the keyboard to another:-

## OH, LONESOME ME (page 30, bars 12 and 13)

bar 12          bar 13

new hand position

half (minim) rest
(use the break to move down to the
new hand position)

# WALTZ TIME

So far all our songs have been in four-time ( $\frac{4}{4}$ ). However, many popular songs have THREE beats to the bar, rather than four. Songs in $\frac{3}{4}$ time (3 "quarter notes" per bar), are called "Waltzes". *Tales Of The Unexpected*, on page 32, is a waltz.

# BLOWIN' IN THE WIND

Words & Music by Bob Dylan

**Suggested registration:** oboe

**Rhythm:** 8 beat
**Tempo:** medium ($\quad$ = 104)
Synchro-start: on

* The **VERSE** is that part of the song which contains the bulk of the narrative. It is usually sung by a solo singer.

sand?
1 2 3 4 1 2 3 4 1 2 3 4

Yes, 'n' how ma - ny

times must the can - non - balls_____ fly, be -
1 2 3 4 1 2 3 4 1 2 3 4

fore they're for - ev - er banned?
1 2 3 4 1 2 3 4 1 2 3 4

The an - swer, my friend, is
1 2 3 4 1 2 3 4 1 2 3 4

blow - in' in the wind, the an - swer is
1 2 3 4 1 2 3 4 1 2 3 4

blow - in' in the wind.
1 2 3 4 1 2 3 4 1 2 3 4

** **CHORUS:** That part of the song where everybody joins in.

# OH, LONESOME ME

Words & Music by Don Gibson

**Suggested registration:** violin

**Rhythm:** swing
**Tempo:** fast ( ♩ = 176 )
Synchro-start: on

A bad mis - take I'm mak - in' by just

hang - in' 'round, _____ I know that I should

have some fun, and paint the town. _____ A

new hand position — stretch — F

love - sick fool that's blind and just can't see. _____

new hand position

Oh, _____ lone - some me. _____

new hand position

stop rhythm

Oh, _____ lone - some me. _____

# NEW RIGHT HAND NOTE: D

NEW NOTE

## TALES OF THE UNEXPECTED
## (Theme from)

By Ron Grainer

**Suggested registration:** marimba (or harpsichord)

**Rhythm:** waltz
**Tempo:** fast ( ♩ = 192)
Synchro-start: on

new hand position

# EIGHTH NOTES (QUAVERS)

The eighth note, or quaver, is another sort of time note:-

eighth notes (quavers)

Eighth notes move twice as fast as your basic quarter note (crotchet) beat:-

In other words, each eighth note is worth HALF A BEAT. If you say the word "and" in between your beat numbers you will get the feel of the eighth note:-

example:-

count: 1      2      3      4      1  and  2  and  3  and  4  and

Keep your basic beats very regular here, then fit the quaver notes *exactly* in between them.

Like all the other time notes, the eighth note has its own rest:-

| eighth (quaver) rest | equivalent to | lasting |
|---|---|---|
|  | ♪ | 1/2 beat |

Count eighth "rests" in exactly the same way that you would count eighth notes:-

## SUPER TROUPER (page 35)

count: 1  and  2  and  3     4      1      2      3  and  4  and

# SUPER TROUPER

Words & Music by Benny Andersson and Bjorn Ulvaeus

**Suggested registration:** trumpet

**Rhythm:** rock
**Tempo:** medium ( ♩ = 104)
Synchro-start: on

# ANNIE'S SONG

Words & Music by John Denver

**Suggested registration:** flute

**Rhythm:** waltz
**Tempo:** medium ( ♩ = 120)
Synchro-start: on

play these two notes together

# 17 LEGATO AND STACCATO

As you know, LEGATO means "joined up", or "connected". When you play legato, you move smoothly from finger to finger, leaving no gaps between notes.

Notes which are to be played legato are indicated on the music by a curved line, called a "slur", or "phrase mark":-

## BIRDIE SONG / BIRDIE DANCE (page 39)

**SLUR**
(play legato)

When there are no slurs, or other markings to the contrary, play LEGATO.

STACCATO means "cut short". It is the opposite of "legato". Release the note as soon as you have played it, using a "pecking" movement of the hand. Notes which are to be played staccato are indicated on the music by dots above, or below the note(s):-

## BIRDIE SONG / BIRDIE DANCE (page 39)

**STACCATO DOTS**
(cut the notes short)

# BIRDIE SONG / BIRDIE DANCE

Words & Music by Werner Thomas and Terry Rendall

**Suggested registration:** banjo

**Rhythm:** cha-cha (or rock)
**Tempo:** medium ( ♩ = 120)
Synchro-start: on

# NEW RIGHT HAND NOTES: E, F, G

┌ NEW NOTES ┐

## LA BAMBA

Adapted and arranged by Ritchie Valens

**Suggested registration:** flute

**Rhythm:** latin (or samba)
**Tempo:** fairly fast ( ♩ = 132)
Synchro-start: on

\* The **VERSE** is that part of the song which contains the bulk of the narrative. It is usually sung by a solo singer.

re por ti se re se re.
1   2 and 3  .  4   1   2   3   4

Yo no soy mar-i-
1   2 and 3   4 and

ne - ro.
1   2   3   4

Yo no soy mar-i- ne - ro, soy cap-i-
1   2 and 3   4 and  1   2 and 3   4

squeeze together

stretch

change finger

flute to brass ensemble

tan. Yo no soy mar-i- ne - ro, soy cap-i- tan.
1   2 and 3   4 and  1   2 and 3   4   1   2   3   4

CHORUS**

stretch

stretch

Bam - ba,      bam - ba.           Bam - ba,
1   2   3   4   1   2   3 and 4 and  1   2   3   4

bam - ba.       Bam - ba,       bam - ba.
1   2   3 and 4 and  1   2   3   4   1   2   3 and 4 and

(If no foot volume pedal available, finish here)

Repeat and Fade

Bam - ba,      bam - ba.
1   2   3   4   1   2   3 and 4 and

**CHORUS: That part of the song where everybody joins in.

# 19 SEVENTH CHORDS

The three chords you have played so far: C , G , and F , are all "major" chords. SEVENTH chords are variations of major chords. When using the "single-finger" chord method, there are various ways of forming "sevenths". Your Owner's Manual will tell you exactly how to form 7ths on your particular instrument, but the first two diagrams below show two possibilities:-

## CHORD OF G 7

Using single-finger chord method – SINGLE-FINGER CHORDS: ON

OR

**Play G, together with any white note to its LEFT.**

**Play G, together with any two notes to its RIGHT.**

Using fingered chord method:- FINGERED CHORDS: ON

# CHORD OF D 7

Using single-finger chord method – SINGLE-FINGER CHORDS: ON

OR

**Play D, together with any white note to its LEFT.**

**Play D, together with any two notes to its RIGHT.**

Using fingered chord method – FINGERED CHORDS: ON

* Sharps and flats will be explained in Book Two. For now simply play the black note indicated.

# SOMETIMES WHEN WE TOUCH

Words & Music by Dan Hill and Barry Mann

**Suggested registration:** oboe

**Rhythm:** 8 beat
**Tempo:** fairly slow ( ♩ = 92)
Synchro-start: on

CHORUS

see the real _____ you. And some - times when we

touch the ho - nest - y's too much, and I

have to close my eyes and hide. _____

_____ I wan - na hold you till I die, till we

both break down and cry. I wan - na hold you till the

fear in me sub - sides. _____

# DAL SEGNO AL FINE (D.S. al Fine)

**DAL SEGNO** means "repeat from the sign":- 𝄋

**FINE** is the end of the piece.

**DAL SEGNO AL FINE (D.S. al Fine)** means go back to the sign: 𝄋 and play through the same music as before until you reach the word "Fine". This is where the piece ends.

## I'D LIKE TO TEACH THE WORLD TO SING

Words & Music by Roger Cook, Roger Greenaway, Billy Backer and Billy Davis

**Suggested registration:** vibraphone

**Rhythm:** swing
**Tempo:** medium (♩ = 120)
**Synchro-start:** on

# CONGRATULATIONS

Congratulations on completing Book One of 'The Complete Keyboard Player'.

In Book Two you will:-

- learn about sharps and flats

- increase the range of your melody playing

- learn new left hand chords, including "minor" chords

- experiment with new sounds and rhythms.

Till then your last piece in this book is:-

## LET IT BE

Words & Music by John Lennon and Paul McCartney

**Suggested registration:** piano

**Rhythm:** rock
**Tempo:** slow ( ♩ = 66 )
Synchro-start: on

**For all portable keyboards by *Kenneth Baker*.**

# THE COMPLETE KEYBOARD PLAYER

## OMNIBUS EDITION

# BOOK 2

In Book 2 of The Complete Keyboard
Player you take a giant step forward in
reading musical notation.

Side by side with the single-finger chords,
you continue your study of 'fingered' chords,
by far the most rewarding aspect of
left hand accompaniment playing.

As the book progresses you play more and more
fill-ins, double notes, and chords with your
right hand, which helps give you that
'professional' sound.

Although Book 2 (like Book 1 of the series)
is designed basically as a 'teach yourself' method,
teachers everywhere will find it ideal for training
tomorrow's electronic keyboard players.

The optional matching CD or cassette, on which you
can hear the author playing all the songs
from the book, will help you to learn even faster!

# SHARPS, FLATS, AND NATURALS

This sign is a sharp: ♯

When you see a sharp written alongside a note, play the nearest available key (black or white) to the RIGHT of that note:-

written:

played:

(F)

**Note:** E sharp is simply an alternative way of writing "F".

This sign is a flat: ♭

When you see a flat written alongside a note, play the nearest available key (black or white) to the LEFT of that note:-

written:

played:

(E)

**Note:** F flat is simply an alternative way of writing "E".

When a sharp or flat is written it continues as a sharp or flat right through the bar:-

At the next bar, however, everything returns to normal:-

Apart from at the new bar, a sharp or flat may be cancelled any time by a sign called a "natural", ♮ :-

Look out for sharps, flats, and naturals in the pieces which follow.

# GET BACK

Words & Music by John Lennon & Paul McCartney

**Suggested registration:** electric guitar

**Rhythm:** jazz organ
**Tempo:** medium (♩ = 120)
**Synchro-start:** on

Jo Jo was a man who thought he was a lon - er,
count: 1 and 2 and 3 4   1 and 2 and 3 4 (etc.)

but he knew it could - n't last.   Jo Jo left his home in

Tuc - son, Ar - i - zo - na, for some Cal - i - for - nia grass.   Get back!

change finger on G

Get back!   Get back to where you once be -

longed. ___   Get back!   Get back!   Get

*COMMON TIME. An alternative way of writing $\frac{4}{4}$.

52

back to where you once be - longed___ Sweet Lo - ret - ta Mod - ern

thought she was a wo - man, but she was an - oth - er man.

All the girls a - round her say she's got it com - ing, but she gets it while she

can. Get back! Get back! Get

back to where you once be - longed___ Get back! Get back!

Get back to where you once be - longed. ___

**\*Pause (Fermata).** Hold the note(s) longer than written (at the discretion of the performer).

# FOR ONCE IN MY LIFE

Words by Ronald Miller
Music by Orlando Murden

**Suggested registration:** piano + string ensemble
  Arpeggio optional

**Rhythm:** samba
**Tempo:** medium ( ♩ = 108)
Synchro-start: on

count: 1   2   3   4   1   2 and 3   4 and   1   2 and 3 and 4 (etc.)

For once in my life I have some - one who needs me ___

some - one I've need - ed so long. For once un - a - fraid I can

go where life leads me, and some - how I know I'll be strong. For

once I can touch what my heart used to dream of long be - fore I

knew some - one warm like you would

make my dream come true. For once in my life I won't

let sor-row hurt me ___ not like it's hurt me be-fore. For

once I have some-thing I know won't de-sert me, and I'm not a-lone an-y-

more. For once I can say this is mine, you can take it, ___

long as I know I have love, I can make it, for once in my life I have

stop rhythm

some - one who needs me. ___

# ROCK AROUND THE CLOCK

Words & Music by Max C. Freedman & Jimmy de Knight

**Suggested registration:** trumpet, or saxophone

**Rhythm:** swing
**Tempo:** fairly fast ( ♩ = 160)

Press rhythm start button (ordinary, not synchro) with left hand, as right hand strikes first note. Play through Verse using melody and drums only. Start left hand chords at Chorus.

VERSE

One, two, three o'-clock, four o'-clock rock! Five, six, se'en o'-clock,

count: 1 2 3 and 4 1 and 2 3 4 (etc.)

*f* (loud)

eight o'-clock rock! Nine, ten, 'leven o'-clock, twelve o'-clock rock, we're gon - na

CHORUS

rock a - round the clock to - night! Put your glad rags on,

join me hon, we'll have some fun when the clock strikes one, we're gon - na

rock a - round the clock to - night, we're gon - na rock, rock, rock, till broad day - light, we're gon - na rock, gon - na rock a - round the clock to -

add arpeggio (if available)

night._____ When the clock strikes two,

three and four, if the band slows down we'll yell for more, we're gon - na

rock a - round the clock to - night, we're gon - na rock, rock, rock till

broad day - light, we're gon - na rock, gon - na rock a - round the clock to -

night. *ff* (very loud) stop rhythm

getting louder
(increase your volume pedal,
if you have one.)

**\* ACCENT**

# 2  TWO NEW CHORDS: [C]7 AND [A]7

Using single-finger chord method:

Locate "C" and "A" in the accompaniment section of your keyboard. Convert these notes into [C] 7 and [A] 7 (see Book One, page 42ff., and your owner's manual).

Using fingered chord method:

# 3  A NEW STAGE IN READING MUSIC

Up to now, in order to help you, letter names have appeared beside the written notes. These letters will now be discontinued.

Here's how you can learn the names of the notes:

The stave consists of five lines:-

remember this sentence:

**E**very **G**ood **B**oy **D**eserves **F**ruit

and four spaces:-

remember this word: **F A C E**

Learn the notes on the five lines, and the notes in the four spaces first.
Then learn the "in-between" notes, like this:

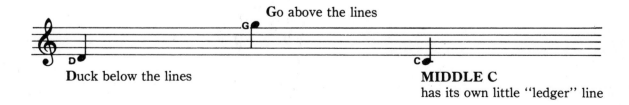

Go above the lines

Duck below the lines

**MIDDLE C**
has its own little "ledger" line

# LOVE ME TENDER

Words & Music by Elvis Presley & Vera Matson

**Suggested registration:** string ensemble
  Arpeggio optional

**Rhythm:** rhumba
**Tempo:** medium ( ♩ = 96)
Synchro-start: on

Love me ten - der, love me sweet, nev - er let me
*p (soft)*

go. You have made my life com - plete,

and I love you so. Love me ten - der,
*crescendo (cresc.)*
*(getting louder by degrees)*

love me true, all my dreams ful - fil.

For, my dar - lin', I love you, and I al - ways will.
*mf (moderately loud)*

# TAKE THESE CHAINS FROM MY HEART

Words & Music by Fred Rose & Hy Heath

**Suggested registration:** guitar

**Rhythm:** 8 beat

**Tempo:** medium (♩ = 108)

Synchro-start: on

Take these chains from my heart and set me free._____

*mp (moderately soft)*

new hand position

___ You've gone cold, and no long - er care for

new hand position

cross 2nd finger over thumb

me. _____ All my faith in you is

*cresc.*

change finger

gone, but the heart - aches ling - er on, take these

*f*

pass thumb under

stop rhythm

chains from my heart and set me free._____

# FORTUOSITY

Words & Music by Richard M. Sherman
& Robert B. Sherman

**Suggested registration:** trombone

**Rhythm:** swing
**Tempo:** fast ( ♩ = 200)
Synchro-start: on

For - tu - os - i - ty,     that's me

by - word,     for - tu - os - i - ty,     the

twin - kle   in   the   eye   word.     Some - times

cas - tles   fall   to   the   ground, _____     but

that's   where   four - leaf   clo - vers   are   found.

*__TENUTO MARK.__ Hold the note for its full length.

For - tu - os - i - ty,

luck - y chan - ces, for - tu -

i - tious lit - tle hap - py hap - pen - stan - ces.

I don't wor - ry, 'cause ev - 'ry - where I

see that ev - 'ry bit of life is lit by

stop rhythm

for - tu - os - i - ty!

*ff*

*GRACE NOTES. Ornamental notes not included in the basic timing of the bar. Play your grace notes as quickly as possible.

# ARE YOU LONESOME TONIGHT

Words & Music by Roy Turk & Lou Handman

**Suggested registration:** flute + full sustain

**Rhythm:** waltz
**Tempo:** fairly slow  ( ♩ = 92)
Synchro-start: on

Are you lone - some to - night, do you

miss me to - night, are you sor - ry we

drift - ed a - part?_____ Does your

mem - or - y stray to a bright sum - mer

tuck thumb under 2nd finger
↓

day, when I kissed you and called you "Sweet -

heart?" Do the chairs in your
*mp cresc.*

par - lour seem emp - ty and bare, do you
*mf*

during rest move 2nd finger up
↓

gaze at the door - step and pic - ture me
*cresc.* *f*

cross 2nd finger
over thumb
↓

there? Is your heart filled with pain? Shall I
*mp* *cresc.*

during rest, move hand up
↓

tuck thumb under
2nd finger
↓

come back a - gain? Tell me dear, are you
*f*

stop rhythm
↓

lone - some to - night?

# 4 STANDARD REPEATING DEVICES

**FIRST AND SECOND TIME BARS:**

| 1. | play these bars on the first time through only. |

| 2. | play this bar on the second time through, then carry on. |

**DA CAPO (D.C.)** — from the beginning.

**DA CAPO AL FINE (D.C. al Fine)** — Go back to the beginning of the piece and play through again until FINE (the end).

## MEMORIES ARE MADE OF THIS

Words & Music by Terry Gilkyson, Richard Dehr & Frank Miller

**Suggested registration:** violin

**Rhythm:** swing
**Tempo:** fairly fast ( ♩ = 144 )
Synchro-start: on

*mf* Take one fresh and ten - der
With some bless - ings from a -

kiss. Add one
bove. Serve it

sto - len night of bliss.
gen - 'rous - ly of with love.

One girl, one boy,
One man, one wife,

some grief, some joy. Me - mo -
one love. through life. Me - mo -

change finger

ries are made of this.
ries are made of this.

(stop rhythm last time)     violin to flute     *(FINE)*

*mp* Then add the wed - ding bells, one house where
Stir care - f'lly through the days, see how the

new hand position

lo - vers dwell, three lit - tle kids for the
fla - vour stays,

1.

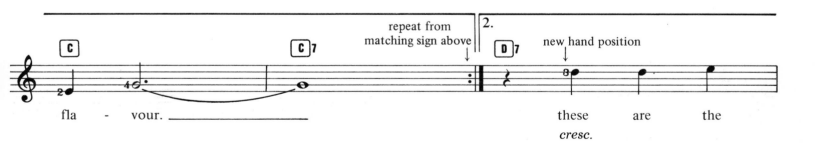

fla - vour. _____ these are the
*cresc.*

repeat from matching sign above     2.     new hand position

dreams you will sa - vour.
*f*

stretch     *D.C. al FINE*
flute to violin

# 5 THREE NEW NOTES FOR RIGHT HAND: LOW G, A, B

These three notes lie directly to the left of Middle C. The lowest of them, G, probably forms the left hand extremity of the "melody section" on your instrument.

I have placed letter names beside the new notes only in the next few songs.

## GUANTANAMERA

Words by Jose Marti
Music adaptation by Hector Angulo & Peter Seeger

**Suggested registration:** pan flute

**Rhythm:** bossa nova
**Tempo:** medium ( ♩ = 112)
Synchro-start: on

cre - ce la pal - ma.___ Yo soy un hom - bre sin - ce - ro___

De don - de cre - ce la pal - ma___ Y an - tes de

change hand position

mo - rir - me quie - ro, E - char mis ver - sos del al -

ma. Guan - ta - na - me - ra___ gua - ji - ra

*f*

Guan - ta - na - me - ra___ Guan - ta - na - me -

ra, gua - ji - ra Guan - ta - na - me - ra!

# CANDLE IN THE WIND

Words & Music by Elton John & Bernie Taupin

**Suggested registration:** clarinet

**Rhythm:** 8 beat
**Tempo:** medium ( ♩ = 120)
Synchro-start: on

VERSE

*mp* Good - bye Nor - ma Jean, ___ though I ne - ver knew you at all, ___

count: 1   2   3   4 and   1   2   3 and 4 and   1   2   3   4 and

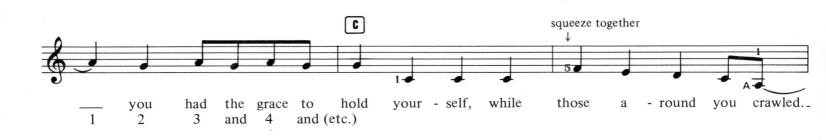

squeeze together

___ you had the grace to hold your - self, while those a - round you crawled..

1   2   3 and 4 and (etc.)

thumb under 2nd finger

They crawled out of the wood - work, ___

___ and they whis - pered in - to your brain, they set you on a

tread - mill, and they made you change your name. ___

70

CHORUS
clarinet to trumpet

And it seems to me you lived your life like a
*mf*

can - dle in the wind, _____ ne - ver know - ing who to

cling to when the rain set in. _____ And I

change finger

would have liked to have known you, but I was just a kid, your

can - dle had burned out long be - fore your le - gend e - ver did. _
*diminuendo (dim.)*
*(getting softer by degrees)*

stop rhythm

*p*

# WHEELS

Words by Norman Petty
Music by Jimmy Torres & Richard Stephens

**Suggested registration:** marimba (or xylophone)

**Rhythm:** cha-cha
**Tempo:** medium (♩ = 116)
**Synchro-start:** on

Wheels go round, and that's how we be-gin it, this, my friend, is

count: 1 2 and 3 4 and 1 2 3 and 4 and 1 2 and 3 4 and

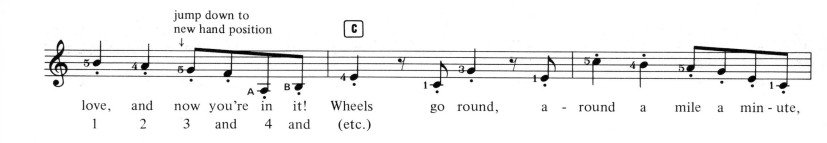

love, and now you're in it! Wheels go round, a - round a mile a min - ute,

1 2 3 and 4 and (etc.)

fun - ny lit - tle wheels in - side your heart! Till it's done, there'll

be no way o' know - in' where you'll run, or why you're all a - glow - in',

one by one, they sim - ply get a - go - in', wheels to spin the wheels that spin your heart! La la la, la la la, la la la, la la

la la. La la la, la la la, la

la la, la la. Wheels go round, but

they don't cost a pen - ny, wheels go round, where once we had -n't a - ny.

Wheels that sound as though there's more than ma - ny, fun - ny lit - tle wheels in - side your

heart! Fun - ny lit - tle wheels in - side your heart!

# MINOR CHORDS

The MINOR CHORD is another important type of chord.

When using the single-finger chord function, there are various ways of forming minor chords. Your owner's manual will tell you how to form minor chords on your particular instrument. The first two diagrams below show two possibilities.

# CHORD OF F MINOR  Fm

Using single-finger chord method:

or:

Play F, together with any black note to its LEFT.

Play F, together with any (one) note to its RIGHT.

Using fingered chord method:

74

# 7 DOTTED TIME NOTES

A dot after a note adds half as much time again to that note:-

|  |  | lasting |
|---|---|---|
| ♩ | half note (minim) | 2 beats |
| ♩. | dotted half note (dotted minim) | 2 + 1 = 3 beats |
| ♩ | quarter note (crotchet) | 1 beat |
| ♩. | dotted quarter note (dotted crotchet) | $1 + \frac{1}{2} = 1\frac{1}{2}$ beats |

# DOTTED QUARTER NOTE (DOTTED CROTCHET)

A Dotted Quarter Note, ♩. , worth $1\frac{1}{2}$ beats, usually combines with an Eighth Note (Quaver), ♪, worth $\frac{1}{2}$ beat, to make two whole beats:-

♩. ♪     $1\frac{1}{2} + \frac{1}{2} = 2$ beats

or:

♪ ♩.     $\frac{1}{2} + 1\frac{1}{2} = 2$ beats

The first of these two time note combinations: ♩. ♪ is the more common. This is how you can count it:-

## WHAT KIND OF FOOL AM I, page 30

Notice how the "dot" delays note D, so that the next note (E) falls on an "and" beat. The situation is always the same with this rhythm.

Look out for other examples of dotted quarter note/quaver combinations in the songs which follow.

# WHAT KIND OF FOOL AM I

Words & Music by Leslie Bricusse & Anthony Newley

**Suggested registration:** *piano & strings*

**Rhythm:** rhumba
**Tempo:** medium ( ♩ = 108)
Synchro-start: on

dwell.

What kind of lips are these that lied with ev - 'ry kiss? That whis - pered emp - ty words of love that left me a - lone like this. Why can't I fall in love like an - y oth - er man, and may - be then I'll know what kind of fool I am.

change piano to horn

change hand position

hold lower notes for 4 beats each

stop rhythm

# LAST OF THE SUMMER WINE

Composed by Ronnie Hazlehurst

**Suggested registration:** harmonica

**Rhythm:** waltz
**Tempo:** medium ($\quarternote$ = 88)
Synchro-start: on

*HIGH A (see page 86).

# STARDUST

Words by Mitchell Parish
Music by Hoagy Carmichael

**Suggested registration:** vibraphone, or celeste,
    + full sustain

**Rhythm:** swing
**Tempo:** fairly slow (♩ = 80)
Synchro-start: on

N.C.  F  stretch

*mp* Some-times I won - der why I spend the lone - ly

count: 1 2 3 and 4 and 1 2 3 4 (etc.)

Fm  C

night dream-ing of a song, the mel - o - dy

A♭7  F

haunts my re - ve - rie. And I am once a - gain with you. When our

G7  C

love was new, and each kiss an in - spi - ra - tion____

D7

— But that was long a - go, now my con - so - la - tion is

*mf*

in     the     star-dust     of     a     song.                    Be  -  side     a     gar  -  den

*mp*

wall     when     stars     are     bright,                    you     are     in     my     arms.     The

night - in - gale     tells     his     fai - ry     tale          of     par - a - dise     where     ro - ses

tuck 5th finger
around 4th
↓

grew.     Tho'     I     dream     in     vain,_____     in     my

*cresc.*

tuck thumb
under 2nd finger
↓

stretch

heart     it     will     re  -  main.                    My          star - dust     mel - o - dy,

*f*

stop rhythm
↓

the     mem - o - ry     of     love's     re  -  frain.

# 8 CHORD OF D MINOR Dm, AND CHORD OF A MINOR Am

Using single-finger chord method:

Locate D (the higher one), and A, in the accompaniment section of your keyboard. Convert these notes into Dm and Am respectively (see page 28 and your owner's manual).

Using fingered chord method:

# SCARBOROUGH FAIR

Traditional

**Suggested registration:** harpsichord

**Rhythm:** waltz
**Tempo:** slow ( ♩ = 88 )
Synchro-start: on

Are you go - ing to Scar - bor - ough

fair? Pars - ley, sage, rose -

ma - ry and thyme_____ Re -

new hand position

mem - ber me to one who lives there.

same as "dim."
(getting softer by degrees)

cross 2nd finger
over thumb

stop rhythm

She once was a true love of mine.

# TAKE ME HOME, COUNTRY ROADS

Words & Music by Bill Danoff, Taffy Nivert & John Denver

**Suggested registration:** electric piano

**Rhythm:** swing
**Tempo:** quite fast ( ♩ = 192)
Synchro-start: on

CHORUS
change electric piano to hawaiian guitar

grow - in' like a breeze.    Coun - try    roads

take me    home    to the

place    I be - long:

West Vir - gin - ia    moun - tain

mom - ma,    take me    home

coun - try    roads.

stop rhythm

If you have a 44, or a 49 note keyboard, these will be your top three notes.

I have placed letter names beside the new notes in the next few songs.

## SAILING

Words & Music by Gavin Sutherland

**Suggested registration:** jazz organ + sustain
**Rhythm:** disco
**Tempo:** slow ( ♩ = 69); but run at double speed ( ♩ = 138)

I am sail - ing,    I am sail - ing,    home a -

gain _____ 'cross the sea.    I am sail - ing storm-y

wa - ters   to be near ___ you,   to be free.   I am

*Pause on each note, for dramatic effect.

86

# SPANISH EYES

Words by Charles Singleton & Eddie Snyder
Music by Bert Kaempfert

**Suggested registration:** steel drums

**Rhythm:** beguine
**Tempo:** medium ( ♩ = 108)
Synchro-start: on

Blue _____ Span - ish
*mp*

eyes, _____ tear - drops are fall - ing
*cresc.*

tuck thumb under 4th finger

from your Span - ish eyes. _____
*mf*

Please _____ please don't cry. _____
*mp*

_____ This is just a - dios and not good
*cresc.*

bye. _____ Soon _____

*mf*  *mp*

___ I'll re - turn, _____

tuck thumb under
3rd finger
↓

squeeze together
↓

bring-ing you all the love your heart can hold. _____

*cresc.*  *f*

tuck 5th finger
around 4th
↓

Please _____ say si

*mp*

si, _____ say you and your Span - ish

*mf*

eyes will wait for me. _____ *f*

stop rhythm

# HOW DEEP IS YOUR LOVE

Words & Music by Barry Gibb, Robin Gibb,
& Maurice Gibb

**Suggested registration:** flute

**Rhythm:** rock
**Tempo:** medium (♩ = 108)
Synchro-start: on

I know your eyes in the morn - ing sun, ___ I feel you touch

___ me in the pour - ing rain. ___ And the mo - ment that you wan - der

far from me, ___ I wan - na feel you in my arms a - gain. ___ And you

come to me ___ on a sum-mer breeze,_ keep me warm in your love, ___ then you

soft - ly leave, and it's me you need to show. ___ How

90

deep is your love?__ How deep is your love? I real - ly mean __ to

learn, ____ 'cause we're liv - ing in a world of fools, ____ break - ing us

new hand position

new hand position

down, when they all should let us be. We be -

cut piano

long to you and me, I be - lieve in you, ____ you know the door __

__ to my ve - ry soul. ____ You're the light ____ in my deep - est

dark - est hour, __ you're my sav - iour when I fall. ____ And you may not think — I care for you, — when you know down in - side — that I

real - ly do. And it's me you need to show. — How

add piano

CHORUS

deep is your love? — How deep is your love? I real -ly mean — to

learn, ——— 'cause we're liv - ing in a world of fools, — break - ing us

down, when they all should let us be. We be - long to you and

play 3 times

stop rhythm

me.

# HELLO GOODBYE

Words & Music by John Lennon & Paul McCartney

**Suggested registration:** synth brass

**Rhythm:** rock
**Tempo:** medium ( ♩ = 112)
Synchro-start: on

You say yes___ I say no___ you say stop___ and

I say go___ go go Oh___

no. You say good - bye, and I say hel -

lo, Hel - lo, hel - lo. I don't know why you say good-bye, I say hel -

lo, Hel - lo, hel - lo. I don't know why you say good-bye, I say hel - lo.

# 10 LAST WORD

Congratulations on reaching the end of Book Two of 'The Complete Keyboard Player'.

In Book Three you will:

- improve your note reading
- learn new chords
- play in new keys, including "minor" keys
- develop further your sense of rhythm
- add those important professional touches to your playing.

## CHORD CHART (Showing all "fingered chords" used in the course so far)

**For all portable keyboards by *Kenneth Baker*.**

# THE COMPLETE KEYBOARD PLAYER

## OMNIBUS EDITION

# BOOK 3

In Book 3 of The Complete
Keyboard Player you learn about scales
and keys. When you play in different
keys you make basic changes of sound,
and so add a new dimension to your
playing. Minor keys, especially, can
change the whole flavour of your music.
In Book 3 you play in five new keys,
including two minor keys.

In Book 3 you continue your left
hand studies, with the emphasis as usual
on 'fingered' chords. Nine new chords
are introduced, in easy stages, and all the
chords used in the series appear in
the Chord Chart at the back of the book.

There is plenty for your right hand in
Book 3. There are double notes,
chords, fill-ins and counter-melodies.

As usual, throughout the book you will
get tips on how to use the facilities of the
keyboard – the sounds, the rhythms, and
so on – more effectively.

Although Book 3 continues in the
'teach yourself' tradition of the earlier
books, all teachers of the instrument will
want to make it one of their standard
text books.

The optional matching CD or cassette, on which you
can hear the author playing all the songs
from the book, will help you to learn even faster!

# CHORD OF E 7

Using single-finger chord method:

Locate "E" (the higher one of two) in the accompaniment section of your keyboard. Convert this note into E 7 (see Book One, page 42ff., and your owner's manual).

Using fingered chord method:

## THE WINNER TAKES IT ALL

Words & Music by Benny Andersson & Bjorn Ulvaeus

**Suggested registration:** piano

**Rhythm:** rock
**Tempo:** medium ( ♩ = 112 )
Synchro-start: on

VERSE
N.C.

I don't wan - na talk a - bout things we've
cards and that's what you've

_mp_

gone through
done too

though it's hurt - ing me
no - thing more to say

now it's his-to---ry._____ I've played all my
no more ace to_____play._____

CHORUS

2. change piano to brass ensemble

The win-ner takes it all, the lo-ser stand-ing

small be-side the vic-to-ry,_____

that's her des-ti---ny._____ The game is on a-

gain, a lov-er or a friend,

a big thing or a small_____ the win-ner takes it

all.

# I LEFT MY HEART IN SAN FRANCISCO

Words by Douglas Cross
Music by George Cory

**Suggested registration:** string ensemble

**Rhythm:** swing
**Tempo:** fairly slow (♩ = 96)
Synchro-start: on

# CHORD OF E MINOR Em

Using single-finger chord method:

Locate "E" (the higher one of two) in the accompaniment section of your keyboard.
Convert this note into Em (see Book Two, page 28, and your owner's manual).

Using fingered chord method:

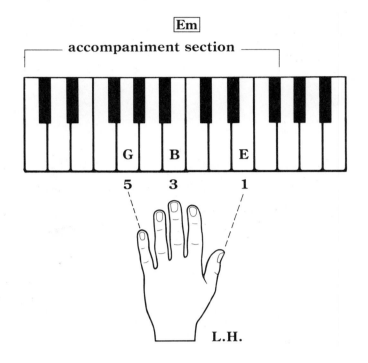

## BRIGHT EYES

Words & Music by Mike Batt

**Suggested registration:** electric guitar + arpeggio

**Rhythm:** rock
**Tempo:** medium ( ♩ = 96)
Synchro-start: on

Is it a kind of a dream.___
fog a - long the ho - ri - zon.

Float - ing out on the tide.___
Cold sound in the air.___

# THE SONG FROM "MOULIN ROUGE"

## (WHERE IS YOUR HEART?)

Words by William Engvick
Music by Georges Auric

**Suggested registration:** hawaiian guitar

**Rhythm:** waltz
**Tempo:** slow ( ♩ = 88)
Synchro-start: on

When - ev - er we kiss, I
*mp*

wor - ry and won - der, your lips may be

here, but ___ where is your heart? It's

al - ways like this, I wor - ry and

won - der, you're close to me here, but ___

*Split these two notes (playing lower note first).

where is your heart? It's a sad thing to re - al -

ise that you've a heart that nev - er melts. _____ When we

kiss do you close your eyes, pre - tend - ing that I'm some - one

else? You must break the spell, this

*mf*       *mp*

cloud that I'm un - der, so please won't you

tell, dar - ling, where is your heart?

*mf*

# SCALE OF C; KEY OF C

A scale is a succession of adjoining notes:

### Scale of C (major)

As you see, there are no black notes in the scale of C.

When a piece is built on this scale it is said to be in the "key of C".
Almost all the pieces you have played so far have been in the key of C.
The occasional black notes you encountered in those pieces were of
a temporary nature only, and did not affect the overall key.

From now on you are going to play in a number of different keys for the sake
of contrast.

# SCALE OF F; KEY OF F

### Scale of F (major)

As you see, a B Flat is required to form the scale of F. When you are playing in
this key, therefore, you must remember to play all your B's, wherever they might
fall on the keyboard, as B Flats.

To remind you, a B Flat is inserted at the beginning of every line:-

**key signature**

To help you further, I have arrowed the first few B Flats in the following songs.

# CHORD OF B♭; CHORD OF F7

You need these two chords in order to play in the Key of F.

Using single-finger chord method:

Locate "B♭" in the accompaniment section of your keyboard. Play this note on its own and you will have a chord of B♭ (major).

Locate "F" (the lower one of two) in the accompaniment section of your keyboard. Convert this into F7 (see Book One, page 42ff., and your owner's manual).

Using fingered chord method:

# OB-LA-DI, OB-LA-DA

Words & Music by John Lennon & Paul McCartney

**Suggested registration:** funny

**Rhythm:** swing
**Tempo:** fast ( ♩ = 112)
Synchro-start: on

VERSE

Des - mond has a bar - row in the

mar - ket place _____ Mol - ly is the

sing - er in a band. _____

Des - mond says to Mol - ly, Girl, I like your face _____

_____ and Mol - ly says this as she takes him by the

*Cut Common Time. A feeling of two in a bar (²/₂) rather than four (⁴/₄).
Notice the metronome marking: ♩ = 112.

CHORUS

hand _____ Ob la di, ob la

*ff*

da, life goes on, bra,

la la how the life goes on. _____

___ Ob la di, ob la da, life goes

on, bra, la la how the

stop rhythm

life goes on.

# FALLING

Words & Music by Angelo Badalamenti & David Lynch

**Suggested registration:** guitar
**Rhythm:** rock
**Tempo:** slow ( ♩ = 100)
Synchro-start: on

Don't let your-self be hurt this time.

Then     I     saw     your
Then     I     saw     your

face.
smile

The   sky ___   is   still   blue, ___   the

clouds come ___ and go, but some - thing ___ is

diff - 'rent, ___ are we fall - ing in

*p cresc.*

love?

*mf*

CHORUS

Fall - ing, fall - ing,

fall - ing, fall - ing in love.

*(Repeat and Fade)*

# TULIPS FROM AMSTERDAM

English Words by Gene Martyn
Original Words by Neumann and Bader
Music by Ralf Arnie

**Suggested registration:** accordion

**Rhythm:** waltz
**Tempo:** fast (♩ = 184)
Synchro-start: on

wait un - til the day you fill

these emp - ty arms of mine. Like the
*mp*

wind - mill keeps on turn - ing, that's how

my heart keeps on yearn - ing, for the

day I know we can _____ share these
*f*

Tu - lips from Am - ster - dam.
*ff*

# TRIPLETS

**4**

A triplet is a group of 3 notes played in the time of 2:-

Eighth Note (Quaver) Triplets must be played slightly FASTER than normal eighth notes, in order to fit them to the beat. Compare the following two examples:-

ex. 1                                    normal eighth notes (quavers)

count:   1   and   2   and   3   and   4   and

ex. 2                                    eighth note (quaver) triplets

count:   1 trip - let   2 trip - let   3 trip - let   4 trip - let
(say aloud)

If you incorporate the word "triplet" into your counting like this, you will get the feeling of the triplets.

# SIXTEENTH NOTES (SEMIQUAVERS), AND DOTTED RHYTHMS

An eighth note (quaver) can be subdivided into two sixteenth notes (semiquavers):-

eighth note   sixteenth notes

A "dotted" eighth note is equal to half as much again (see "dotted time notes", Book Two, page 29), that is, three sixteenth notes:-

dotted eighth note    sixteenth notes

In practice, a dotted eighth note usually pairs up with a sixteenth note:-

dotted eighth note  sixteenth note

Together these two time notes are equivalent to 4 sixteenth notes, or 1 quarter note (crotchet):-

3 sixteenth notes + 1 sixteenth note  =  quarter note

The general effect of a passage like:-

is of eighth notes (quavers) with a "lilt". The phrase "humpty dumpty" can be used as a guide to this rhythm:-

say:  hump - ty dump - ty hump - ty dump - ty
stress

These uneven types of rhythms are often called "Dotted Rhythms". Look out for dotted rhythms in the next four pieces.

In *Close To You*, watch out for "normal" eighth notes, eighth note triplets, and dotted rhythms.

# (THEY LONG TO BE) CLOSE TO YOU

Words by Hal David. Music by Burt Bacharach

**Suggested registration:** piano

**Rhythm:** swing
**Tempo:** medium ( ♩ = 96)
Synchro-start: on

Why do birds sud-den-ly ap-pear ev-'ry
why all the boys in town fol-low
count: 1 2 3 4-trip-let

time you are near?
you all a-round.
1 2 3 4-trip-let
Just like me ___
Just like me ___

they long to be close to you. ___ Why do
they long to be

stars fall down from the sky ev-'ry time you walk by?

Just like me ___ they long to be close to you. ___

add string ensemble

114

On the day that you were born the an-gels got to-ge-ther and de-
(say) hump-ty dump-ty hump-ty dump-ty

ci-ded to cre-ate a dream come true, so they sprink-led moon-dust in your hair of

gold, and star-light in your eyes of blue. That is

close to you. Ah,

close to you.

*A **CODA** is a section, usually quite short, added to a piece of music to make an ending.
**DAL SEGNO AL CODA** (*D.S. al CODA*) means go back to the sign: 𝄉 and play through the same music again, until: "*to CODA* ⊕". From here jump to *CODA* and play through to the end.

# 5 SCALE OF G; KEY OF G

**Scale of G (major)**

G  A  B  C  D  E  (F♯)  G

An F Sharp is required to form the scale of G. When a piece is built on this scale it is said to be in the "key of G". When you are playing in this key you must remember to play all Fs, wherever they might fall on the keyboard, as F Sharps. The key signature, which appears at the beginning of every line, will remind you:-

key signature        **Key of G**

# CHORD OF [B] 7

Using single-finger chord method:

Locate "B" in the accompaniment section of your keyboard. Convert this into [B] 7 (see Book One, page 42ff., and your owner's manual).

Using fingered chord method:

## CHANSON D'AMOUR

Words & Music by Wayne Shanklin

**Suggested registration:** choir

**Rhythm:** swing
**Tempo:** medium (♩ = 100)
Synchro-start: on

*p* Chan - son d'a - mour _____
Chan - son d'a - mour _____

_____ ra da da da da, play en - core_
_____ ra da da da da, je t'a - dore_

*mf*

# WHEN I'M SIXTY-FOUR

Words & Music by John Lennon & Paul McCartney

**Suggested registration:** clarinet

**Rhythm:** swing
**Tempo:** medium ( ♩ = 112)
Synchro-start: on

When I get old - er, los - ing my hair __ ma - ny __ years from

now, will you still be send - ing me a Val - en - tine __

birth - day greet - ings, bot - tle of wine? __ If I'd been out __ till

quar - ter to three __ would you lock the door?

Will you still need __ me, will you still feed __ me, when I'm six - ty __

four? (stop rhythm last time) *p* Ev - 'ry sum - mer we can rent a cot - tage in the Isle of

Wight, if it's not too dear. We shall

scrimp and save

Ah grand - child - ren on your knee

Ve - ra, Chuck, and

Dave. *f*

*Leave synchro button on, and rhythm will start again automatically when you strike the next chord ("G", at the beginning of the piece).

# CHORDS OF G MINOR Gm, AND B♭ MINOR B♭m

Using single-finger chord method:

Locate "G" and "B♭" in the accompaniment section of your keyboard. Convert these notes into Gm and B♭m respectively (see Book Two, page 28, and your owner's manual).

Using fingered chord method:

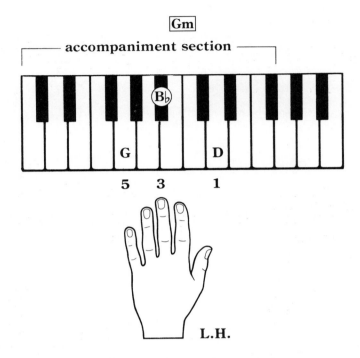

Compare this chord with G (major), a chord you already know.

Compare this chord with B♭ (major), a chord you already know.

# ISN'T SHE LOVELY

Words & Music by Stevie Wonder

**Suggested registration:** piano + sustain
**Rhythm:** swing
**Tempo:** medium ( ♩ = 112)
**Synchro-start:** on

**\*QUARTER NOTE (CROTCHET) TRIPLET.** 3 quarter notes played in the time of 2. Play these quarter notes slightly faster than usual, in order to fit them into the bar, but keep them even, and equal to each other.

# (EVERYTHING I DO) I DO IT FOR YOU

Words & Music by Bryan Adams, R.J. Lange and M. Kamen

**Suggested registration:** flute

**Rhythm:** 8 beat
**Tempo:** slow (♩ = 80)
Synchro-start: on

Look in - to my eyes, you will see _____ what you mean to

*mp*

me. Search your heart, _____ search your soul, _____ and when you

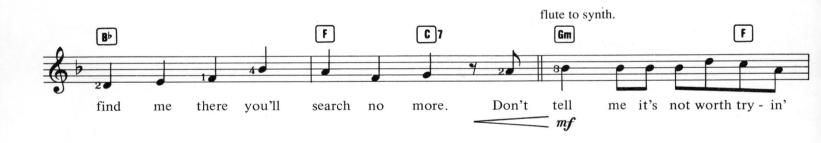

flute to synth.

find me there you'll search no more. Don't tell me it's not worth try - in'

_____ *mf*

for. You can't tell me it's not worth dy - in' for. You know it's

true, _____ ev - 'ry - thing I do, I do it for _____ you

*p*

synth. to flute

Look in - to your heart, you will find ____ no - thin' there to hide. Take me
*mp*

flute to synth.

as I am, take my life, ____ I would give it all I would sac - ri - fice. You can't

tell me it's not worth try - in' for. I can't help ____ it there's no - thin' I want
*mf*

more. Yeah, I would fight for you, I'd lie for you. Walk the

stop rhythm (then synchro-start on)
synth. to flute
(rhythm starts)

wire for you, ____ yeah, I'd die for you, you know it's true, ev -'ry-thing I
*f   mp*

stop rhythm

do, oh, ____ I do it for ____ you. ____
*mf*

# 7 MINOR KEYS

So far almost all your playing has been in major keys: C, F, and G. Songs written in minor keys, with their preponderance of minor chords, often have a sad, nostalgic quality, which makes an excellent contrast.

## KEY OF D MINOR

The key of D Minor is related to the key of F Major. The scales on which these keys are built use the same notes:

**Scale of D Minor ('natural')**                **Scale of F**

D  E  F  G  A (B♭) C  D

F  G  A (B♭) C  D  E  F

All the notes are white except one: B Flat. As you would expect, both keys have the same key signature:

**Key of D Minor**                              **Key of F**

When playing in the key of D Minor (as in the key of F), you must remember to play all B's, wherever they might fall on the keyboard, as B Flats.

# SUNNY

Words & Music by Bobby Hebb

**Suggested registration:** *jazz organ, with stereo chorus.*

**Rhythm:** rock
**Tempo:** medium ( ♩ = 96)
Synchro-start: on

Sun - ny
*mp*
yes - ter - day my life was filled with

rain._____ Sun - ny you smiled at me and

real - ly eased the pain,_____ oh the dark days are done and the
*cresc.*

bright days are here, my Sun - ny one shines so sin - cere,___ oh, Sun - ny one so
*mf*

1.

2.

true, I love you._____
*f*
*f*

# HAVA NAGILA

Traditional

**Suggested registration:** bass clarinet

**Rhythm:** march $\frac{2}{4}$ (or swing)

**Tempo:** medium ( ♩ = 112)

(Speed up tempo control, bit by bit, with left hand)

Change bass clarinet to harpsichord 2nd time

(leave tempo control now)

Stop rhythm

# KEY OF E MINOR

8

The key of E Minor is related to the key of G Major. Both keys use the same scale notes:

### Scale of E Minor ('natural')

E (F♯) G A B C D E

### Scale of G

G A B C D E (F♯) G

All the notes are white except one: F Sharp.

The key signature is the same for both keys:

### Key of E Minor

### Key of G

When playing in the key of E Minor (as in the key of G), you must remember to play all F's, wherever they might fall on the keyboard, as F Sharps.

# CALLAN (SOGNO NOSTALGICO)

By Armando Sciascia

**Suggested registration:** *guitar*

**Rhythm:** waltz
**Tempo:** slow ( ♩ = 88)
Synchro-start: on

tuck 5th finger
around 4th

N.C.
stop rhythm

*rit.*
(slowing down gradually)

*mf*

# A WOMAN IN LOVE

Words & Music by Barry Gibb & Robin Gibb

**Suggested registration:** flute

**Rhythm:** 8 beat
**Tempo:** medium (♩ = 96)
Synchro-start: on

1. Life is a mo-ment in space,___ when the dream is gone,___ it's a lone-li-er place.___
2. With you e-ter-nal-ly mine,___ in love there is___ no___ mea-sure of time.___

*mp*

I kiss the morn-ing good-bye,___ but down in-side___
We planned it all at the start,___ that you and I___

*cresc.*

___ you know we ne-ver know why.___ The road is nar-row and long,___
___ live in each oth-er's heart.___ We may be o-ceans a-way,___

*mf*    *mp*

___ when eyes meet eyes,___ and the feel-ing is strong. ___
you feel my love,___ I hear what you say. ___

I turn a-way from the wall,___ I stum-ble and fall,___ but I give you it all.___
The truth is ev-er a lie,___ I stum-ble and fall,___ but I give you it all.___

*cresc.*

130

CHORUS

# 9   KEY OF B FLAT

The scale of B Flat, and therefore the key of B Flat, requires two flats: B Flat, and E Flat:-

**Scale / Key of B Flat (major)**

**key signature**

When you are playing in this key you must remember to play all B's and E's, wherever they might fall on the keyboard, as B Flats and E Flats, respectively.

# CHORD OF E♭ (MAJOR)

Using single-finger chord method:

Play the note "E♭" (the higher one of two) in the accompaniment section of your keyboard.

Using fingered chord method:

# DON'T CRY FOR ME ARGENTINA

Music by Andrew Lloyd Webber
Lyrics by Tim Rice

**Suggested registration:** trumpet

**Rhythm:** tango
**Tempo:** medium ($\quarternote$ = 112)
Synchro-start: on

# MAMMA MIA

Words & Music by Benny Andersson, Stig Anderson
& Bjorn Alvaeus

**Suggested registration:** oboe

**Rhythm:** rock
**Tempo:** medium (♩ = 126)
Synchro-start: on

VERSE

I've been cheat-ed by you___ since I don't know when.
So I made up my mind___ it must come to an end.

*mf*

*mp*

Look at me now___ will I ev - er learn?

*mp*

I don't know how___ but I sud-den-ly lose___ con-trol

There's a fire ___ with - in my soul _____ just a

*f*

look and I can hear a bell ring ___ One more look and I for-get ev-'ry-thing___

CHORUS

Oh _____ Mam-ma Mi - a! Here I go _____ a-gain,

my, my! How can I re-sist you? Mam-ma Mi - a!

Does it show _____ a-gain, my, my! Just how much I've missed you.

Yes _____ I've been bro - ken heart - ed, blue _____ since the day _____

_____ we part - ed, why, why, did I ev - er let _____ you

go?

ff

stop rhythm

135

# CHORD OF C MINOR [Cm]

Using single-finger chord method:

Locate "C" (the higher one of two) in the accompaniment section of your keyboard. Convert this note into [Cm] (see Book Two, page 28, and your owner's manual).

Using fingered chord method:

Compare this chord with [C] (major), a chord you already know.

## RAINDROPS KEEP FALLING ON MY HEAD

Words by Hal David
Music by Burt Bacharach

**Suggested registration:** whistle

**Rhythm:** swing
**Tempo:** medium ($\quarternote$ = 104)
Synchro-start: on

Rain - drops    keep fall - in' on    my    head,
did    me    some talk - in' to    the    sun.

just    like    the guy whose feet are    too    big    for    his    bed,    no - thing seems to
I    said    I    did - n't like the    way    he    got    things    done,    sleep - in' on the

*DA CAPO AL CODA (D.C. al Coda) means go back to the beginning of the piece and play through the same music again, until: "to CODA ⊕". From here jump to CODA and play through to the end.

# STAR WARS (THEME)

By John Williams

**Suggested registration:** brass ensemble

**Rhythm:** disco
**Tempo:** medium (♩ = 112)
Synchro-start: on

# CHORD CHART (Showing all "fingered chords" used in the course so far)

Printed in the United Kingdom by
Redwood Books Limited, Trowbridge, Wiltshire

11/99(35846)

**Big value songbooks...**
**packed with great**
**music for keyboard**
**players, singers,**
**guitar players and**
**all kinds of**
**musicians.**

**The Beatles.**
**100 Hits for All Keyboards**
For the first time a bumper
collection of their greatest
hits arranged for
keyboards. Includes
'Please Please Me',
'A Hard Day's Night',
'The Long And Winding
Road' and 'Lucy In The
Sky With Diamonds'.
With lyrics and suggested
registrations.
*208pp, NO 18590*

**Chris De Burgh.**
**Greatest Hits for**
**All Keyboards.**
Thirty-five of his greatest
songs arranged for piano,
electronic piano, organ and
portable keyboards. Each
song includes chord
symbols, lyrics, suggested
registrations and rhythms.
*136pp, AM 81837*

**Phil Collins.**
**Greatest Hits for**
**All Keyboards.**
His best songs - arranged
for all keyboards. Each
song includes chord
symbols and lyrics. New
arrangements including
suggested registrations
and rhythms.
*118pp, AM 80664*

**100 All-Time Standards**
**for All Keyboards.**
A great collection of songs
with lyrics, registrations
and chord symbols. Titles
include 'A Taste Of Honey',
'Can't Smile Without You',
'I Left My Heart In San
Francisco', 'Send In The
Clowns' and 'You Don't
Bring Me Flowers'.
*230pp, AM 78072*

**Fifty T.V. Themes**
**for All Keyboards.**
Your favourite TV themes
arranged by Daniel Scott.
Each tune includes chord
symbols, registrations and
some lyrics. Titles include
'Allo, Allo', 'Bergerac',
'Coronation Street',
'LA Law', 'Rumpole Of
The Bailey' and the
'Onedin Line'.
*128pp, AM 78932*

**Easy Listening Love & Rock**
**for All Keyboards.**
Fifty best-loved songs in
the soft rock style.
Arranged for all keyboards
and complete with lyrics,
suggested registrations
and tempo settings.
*160pp, AM 83916*

**Available from all good music shops.**

**The bigger the book, the better the value.**

# Bumper Books

**Show Tunes.**
**100 Hits for All Keyboards.**
Arranged by Daniel Scott.
The songs that stopped the
shows, arranged for all
keyboards. Each song
includes chord symbols,
lyrics, performance tips
and suggested
registrations.
*260pp, AM 74105*

**"The Ultimate Keyboard Book"**
**250 All-Time Hits.**
A wonderful collection of
melodies for all keyboard
players. Complete with
registrations, lyrics and
chord symbols.
*144pp, AM 63256*
*140pp, Book 2: AM 69212*

**250 All-Time Hits Book 3**
A third collection of all-time
great songs arranged for all
keyboard players.
Complete with melody
lines, registrations and
chord symbols.
*156pp, AM 80359*

**200 All-Time Show Tunes**
A bumper collection of the
greatest show music, all
presented in easy to play
top line arrangements,
complete with lyrics and
chord symbols. Titles
include 'Consider Yourself',
'I Could Have Danced All
Night', 'Ol' Man River' and
'Sunrise, Sunset'.
*148pp, AM 78643*

**101 Bumper SFX**
**For All Home Keyboards**
A superb collection of 101
songs in many styles, all
arranged in letter-note SFX
notation. Complete with
suggested registrations
and lyrics.
*300pp, AM 78908*

**100 Jazz & Blues Greats**
One hundred of the world's
favourite jazz and blues
classics. Arranged for
piano/vocal with full lyrics
and chord symbols.
*312pp, AM66614*

In case of difficulty, please contact
**Music Sales Limited, Newmarket Road, Bury St Edmunds, Suffolk IP33 3YB**
**Telephone: 0284 702600**

# Bringing you the world's best music.